EXPLORE THE U.S.A.

UTAH

Cindy Rodriguez

www.av2books.com

LET'S READ
AV2
BY WEIGL™
ADDED VALUE • AUDIO VISUAL

Go to **www.av2books.com**, and enter this book's unique code.

BOOK CODE

Q169355

AV² by Weigl brings you media enhanced books that support active learning.

AV² provides enriched content that supplements and complements this book. Weigl's AV² books strive to create inspired learning and engage young minds in a total learning experience.

Your AV² Media Enhanced books come alive with...

Audio
Listen to sections of the book read aloud.

Video
Watch informative video clips.

Embedded Weblinks
Gain additional information for research.

Try This!
Complete activities and hands-on experiments.

Key Words
Study vocabulary, and complete a matching word activity.

Quizzes
Test your knowledge.

Slide Show
View images and captions, and prepare a presentation.

... and much, much more!

Published by AV² by Weigl
350 5th Avenue, 59th Floor
New York, NY 10118
Website: www.av2books.com   www.weigl.com

Library of Congress Cataloging-in-Publication Data
Rodriguez, Cindy.
 Utah / Cindy Rodriguez.
    p. cm. -- (Explore the U.S.A.)
 Audience: Grades K-3.
 Includes bibliographical references and index.
 ISBN 978-1-61913-409-6 (hbk. : alk. paper)
 1. Utah--Juvenile literature. I. Title.
 F826.3.R63 2012
 979.2--dc23
                            2012015032

Printed in the United States of America in North Mankato, Minnesota
1 2 3 4 5 6 7 8 9 0   16 15 14 13 12

052012
WEP040512

Project Coordinator: Karen Durrie
Art Director: Terry Paulhus

Weigl acknowledges Getty Images as the primary image supplier for this title.

UTAH

Contents

3

This is Utah.
It is the Beehive State.
The bee stands for hard work.

This is the shape of Utah. It is in the west part of the United States.

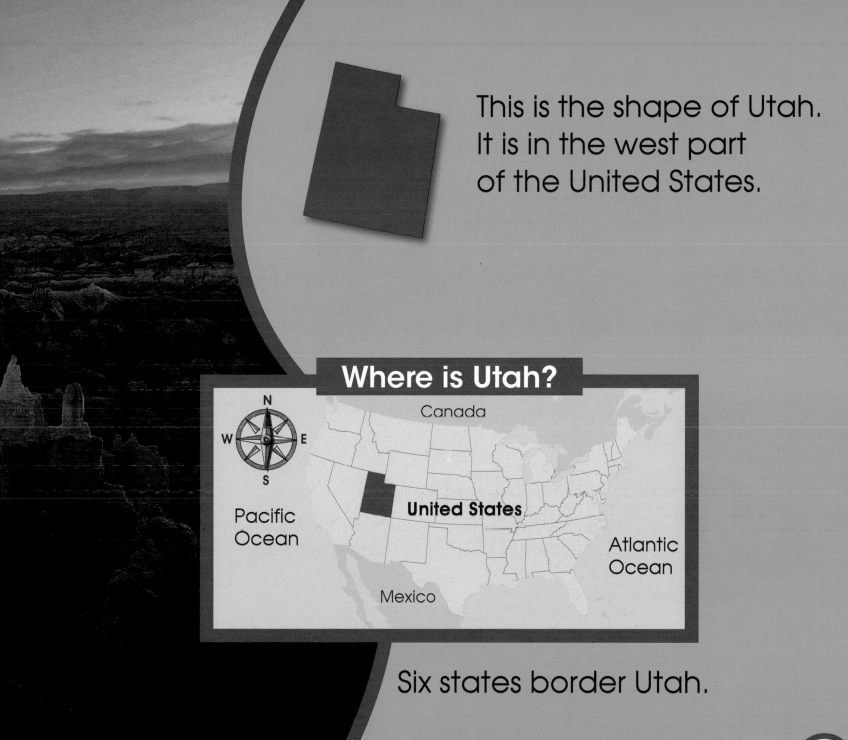

Where is Utah?

Canada

Pacific Ocean

United States

Atlantic Ocean

Mexico

Six states border Utah.

Mormon pioneers came to Utah about 165 years ago. They came in wagons on a road more than 1,000 miles long.

The road they took is now called the Mormon Trail.

The sego lily is the Utah state flower. Early settlers ate the bulbs of the sego lily.

The Utah state seal has a beehive, sego lilies, and two American flags.

A bald eagle is also on the seal.

This is the state flag of Utah.
It is blue with the state seal
in the middle.

The sego lily on the
seal stands for peace.

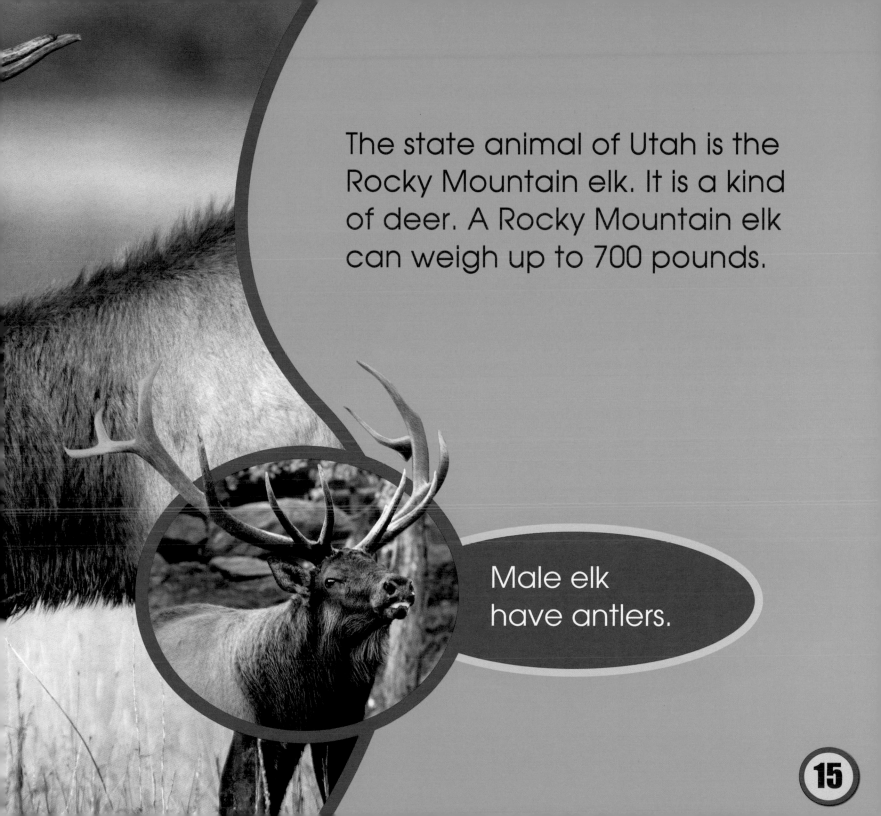

The state animal of Utah is the Rocky Mountain elk. It is a kind of deer. A Rocky Mountain elk can weigh up to 700 pounds.

Male elk have antlers.

This is the largest city in Utah. It is named Salt Lake City. It is the state capital.

The 2002 Winter Olympics were held in Salt Lake City.

SALT LAKE 2002

Utah has many cows. Some cows make milk. Milk can be used to make other foods.

In one year, Utah cows made about 1.9 billion pounds of milk.

Utah is known for its mountains, lakes, rivers, and deserts.

People come to Utah to ski in the winter, and hike and bike in the summer.

21

UTAH FACTS

These pages provide detailed information that expands on the interesting facts found in the book. These pages are intended to be used by adults as a learning support to help young readers round out their knowledge of each state in the *Explore the U.S.A.* series.

Pages 4–5

Utah's nickname, the Beehive State, comes from the state's original name. It was called Deseret, a word meaning, "Land of the Honeybee." The beehive is a symbol of the people of Utah and their hard work and industry. Utah's name comes from the Europeans, who called the area the land of the Utes, an American Indian tribe living there.

Pages 6–7

On January 4, 1896, Utah joined the United States as the 45th state. Utah is bordered by Idaho and Wyoming to the north, Arizona and New Mexico to the south, Colorado and Wyoming to the east, and Nevada to the west. Four Corners is found in southeast Utah. It is the only place where four states meet at one point.

Pages 8–9

In 1847, Mormons arrived in the Salt Lake Valley. Many had left Illinois and Missouri because their beliefs were not accepted. Mormon leader Brigham Young led his people west in search of a place where they could live in peace. Before the railroad reached Utah in 1869, about 70,000 Mormons used the Mormon Trail to reach the state.

Pages 10–11

The sego lily was voted state flower in 1911. The flower's bulb was important to the early settlers during their first winter when food was scarce. The state seal has an eagle at the top. The six arrows beneath the eagle stand for protection during peace and war.

Pages 12–13

The state seal sits in the middle of the solid blue background. There are two years on the seal. The year 1847 is when the Mormon pioneers arrived in the area. Utah achieved statehood in 1896. The flag was originally designed in 1912 for the battleship *Utah*.

Pages 14–15

Rocky Mountain elk were found all over the United States at one time. Now, they are only found in the western part of the country. Hunting and destruction of habitat reduced their numbers. Male Rocky Mountain elk can weigh up to 700 pounds (318 kilograms).

Pages 16–17

Salt Lake City was named for the Great Salt Lake. It is the largest U.S. lake west of the Mississippi River. The Great Salt Lake is three to five times saltier than the ocean. The 2002 Winter Olympics brought athletes from all over the world to compete in many winter sports, including ski jumping, snowboarding, bobsled, luge, and skating.

Pages 18–19

Utah has more than 11 million acres (4.45 million hectares) of farms. About 85,000 dairy cows produce milk in Utah. Utah dairy products include cheese, yogurt, and ice cream. More than one million gallons (3.8 million liters) of ice cream are made in Utah each month.

Pages 20–21

Utah has many landscapes. The Rocky Mountains, the Great Salt Lake Desert, and the Colorado River are all found in Utah. Visitors enjoy the national parks, colorful canyons, monuments, and ski resorts. In 2010, almost five million people visited Utah's state parks. People enjoy outdoor activities year-round because of Utah's mild winters.

KEY WORDS

Research has shown that as much as 65 percent of all written material published in English is made up of 300 words. These 300 words cannot be taught using pictures or learned by sounding them out. They must be recognized by sight. This book contains 52 common sight words to help young readers improve their reading fluency and comprehension. This book also teaches young readers several important content words, such as proper nouns. These words are paired with pictures to aid in learning and improve understanding.

Page	Sight Words First Appearance
4	for, hard, is, it, state, the, this, work
7	in, of, part, where
8	a, about, came, long, miles, more, now, on, than, they, to, took, years
11	also, American, and, has, two
12	with
15	animal, can, have, kind, up
16	city, named, were
19	be, foods, made, make, many, other, some, used
21	come, its, mountains, people, rivers

Page	Content Words First Appearance
4	bee, beehive, Utah
7	shape, United States
8	pioneers, road, wagons, trail
11	bald eagle, bulbs, flags, flower, seal, sego lily, settlers
12	middle, peace
15	antlers, deer, pounds, Rocky Mountain elk
16	capital, Salt Lake City, Winter Olympics
19	cows, milk
21	deserts, lakes, summer, winter

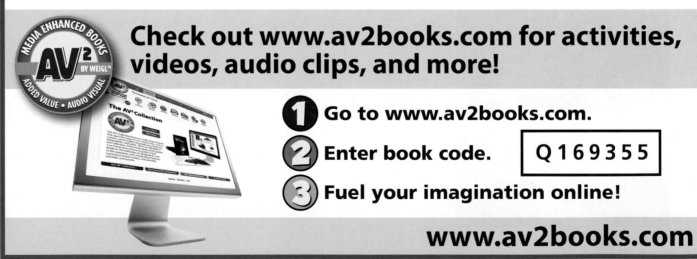